DURHAM COUNTY LIBRARY

Apr 04 2016

DURHAM NC

SUPERHEROES OF SCIENCE

STEPHEN HAWKING

MASTER OF THE COSMOS

Robert Snedden

Gareth Stevens
PUBLISHING

Please visit our website, **www.garethstevens.com**. For a free color catalog of all our high-quality books, call toll free 1-800-542-2595 or fax 1-877-542-2596.

Library of Congress Cataloging-in-Publication Data

Sneddon, Robert.
Stephen Hawking: master of the cosmos / by Robert Sneddon.
p. cm. – (Superheroes of science)
Includes index.
ISBN 978-1-4824-3157-5 (pbk.)
ISBN 978-1-4824-3160-5 (6 pack)
ISBN 978-1-4824-3158-2 (library binding)
1. Hawking, Stephen, – 1942- – Juvenile literature. 2. Physicists – Great Britain – Biography – Juvenile literature. 3. Scientists – Great Britain – Biography – Juvenile literature. I. Sneddon, Robert. II. Title.
QC16.H33 D53 2016
539.092–d23
First Edition

Published in 2016 by
Gareth Stevens Publishing
111 East 14th Street, Suite 349
New York, NY 10003

Produced for Gareth Stevens by Calcium
Editors for Calcium: 3REDCARS
Designers: Paul Myerscough and 3REDCARS

Picture credits: Cover art by Mat Edwards; Dreamstime: Alexanderphoto7 43c, Arindam Banerjee 38c, Featureflash 37c, Thomas Jurkowski 32t, PixelParticle 39t, Science Pics 44t, Shatungoo 21t; Shutterstock: Fernando Batista 23t, Benmoat 10–11, Bildagentur Zoonar GmbH 17t, J. Henning Buchholz 12c, Catwalker 17c, Chaoss 2c, Ivan Cholakov 7t, David Fowler 5c, Julietphotography 11t, Jupeart 15t, Georgios Kollidas 6b, Vadim Sadovski 19t; Wikimedia Commons: 28c, 29c, Anzenbergergallery 10b, Biswarup Ganguly 40c, Intel Free Press 25c, Ute Kraus 41t, NASA 15c, 24c, 26c, 31c, 43t, National Archives and Records Administration 9t, A. T. Service 25t, Doug Wheller 36c.

Printed in the United States of America
CPSIA compliance information: Batch #CS15GS: For further information contact Gareth Stevens, New York, New York at 1-800-542-2595.

CONTENTS

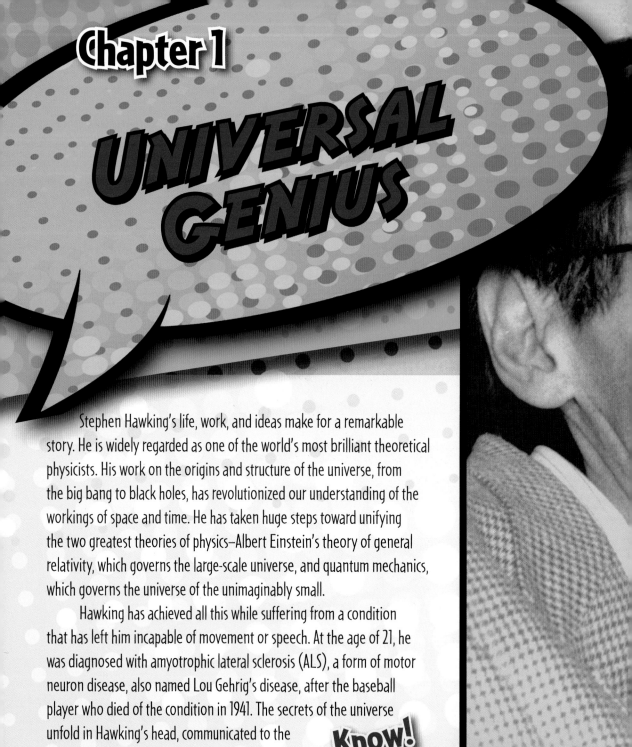

Chapter 1

UNIVERSAL GENIUS

Stephen Hawking's life, work, and ideas make for a remarkable story. He is widely regarded as one of the world's most brilliant theoretical physicists. His work on the origins and structure of the universe, from the big bang to black holes, has revolutionized our understanding of the workings of space and time. He has taken huge steps toward unifying the two greatest theories of physics—Albert Einstein's theory of general relativity, which governs the large-scale universe, and quantum mechanics, which governs the universe of the unimaginably small.

Hawking has achieved all this while suffering from a condition that has left him incapable of movement or speech. At the age of 21, he was diagnosed with amyotrophic lateral sclerosis (ALS), a form of motor neuron disease, also named Lou Gehrig's disease, after the baseball player who died of the condition in 1941. The secrets of the universe unfold in Hawking's head, communicated to the world through a computer and speech synthesizer activated by tiny twitches of a cheek muscle.

Kpow!

Stephen Hawking has become one of the most recognized scientists in the world today.

Celebrity Scientist

Hawking once said, "My goal is simple. It is a complete understanding of the universe, why it is as it is and why it exists at all." He has probably come as close as any scientist to achieving this understanding. In the process, he has become perhaps the best-known scientist since Albert Einstein and has made science much more popular, talked about, and understood.

STAR CONTRIBUTION

Now in his 70s, Hawking still carries out his research into theoretical physics and travels the world to give lectures on his findings. He also has great ambitions to make it into space one day and perhaps also to have his brain encoded onto a computer. Speaking at the premiere of a documentary movie about his life in 2013, he said, "I think the brain is like a program in the mind, which is like a computer, so it's theoretically possible to copy the brain onto a computer and so provide a form of life after death."

BORN IN WARTIME

Stephen William Hawking was born January 8, 1942. This was the 300th anniversary of the death of the great Italian scientist Galileo, who first used a telescope to observe the moons of Jupiter and the craters of the moon. Hawking is quite proud of this shared anniversary.

Hawking's parents lived in Highgate, in north London, England. When Hawking was due to be born, it was the middle of World War II, and the German airforce was carrying out regular bombing raids on London. Hawking's father, Frank, decided London was far too hazardous a place to be when his wife gave birth and moved his family to the relative safety of Oxford. It was there that Stephen Hawking was born.

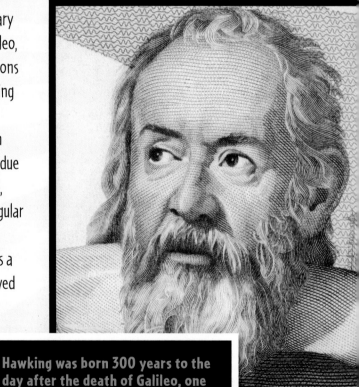

Hawking was born 300 years to the day after the death of Galileo, one of the fathers of modern physics.

Future Vision!

A few days before Stephen was born, his mother, Isobel, went into a bookstore and bought an atlas of astronomy. Later she liked to think that she had a premonition about how her son would turn out!

SUPERHERO FACT

Bomber planes were a familiar sight over London around the time that Hawking was born.

Isobel Hawking, Stephen's mother, had graduated from the University of Oxford, where she studied economics, philosophy, and politics. Oxford had only been granting degrees to women since 1920, and the 1930s, when Isobel was a student, were a time when few women went to university. Stephen's father, who had studied medical science, was also an Oxford graduate. Neither of their families were wealthy and both had struggled to find the money to send their children to university.

Hawking's parents met at a medical institute in London, where Isobel was a medical secretary and Frank was a respected medical researcher, specializing in tropical diseases. They were married just after the war started. Hawking's first sister, Mary, was born 18 months after he was, and his other sister, Philippa, was born when he was nearly 5. Hawking describes her as a "very perceptive child" and says that he has always respected her judgment and opinions. Hawking also has a brother, Edward, who was adopted by the family when Hawking was 14.

FIRST SCHOOL DAYS

The Hawkings returned to Highgate, in London, soon after Stephen was born. The war was still going on and London could be dangerous. On one occasion, just after the birth of Mary Hawking, the family had a lucky escape when a German rocket exploded near their home. Sharp shards of glass blew in from the back windows and embedded in the wall opposite. Fortunately, only Frank Hawking was in the house and he was unhurt.

Crash!

The German bombing of London hit all parts of the city, including Highgate, where the Hawkings lived.

The war had ended by the time Hawking started going to school, at age four. He attended Byron House School in Highgate, which he describes as "very progressive" for the time. Most of the other children there also had parents who were scientists or academics. Hawking recalls complaining to his parents that he was not learning anything at Byron House—"You were supposed to learn to read without realizing you were being taught." In the end, he did not learn to read until the age of eight. His sister Philippa could read when she was four, but, as Hawking says, "She was definitely brighter than me."

Hawking has said that he and his sister Mary were always rivals, probably because they were so close in age. The competition between them only lessened in adulthood, when they followed very different career paths—Stephen into theoretical physics and his sister into medicine as a doctor.

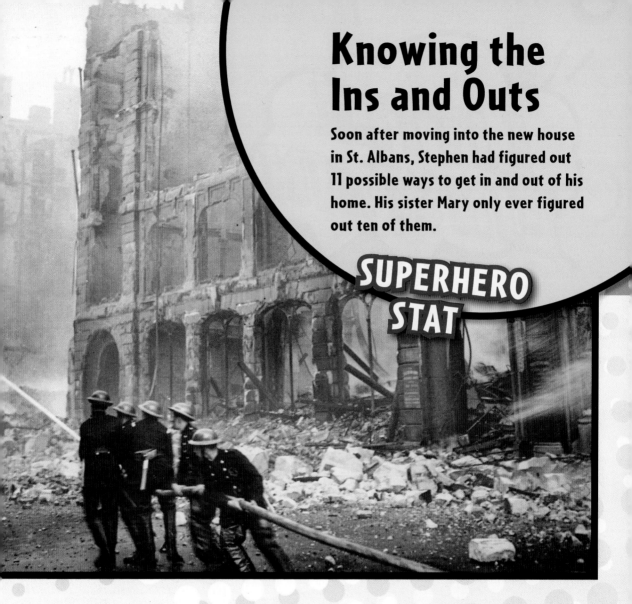

Knowing the Ins and Outs

Soon after moving into the new house in St. Albans, Stephen had figured out 11 possible ways to get in and out of his home. His sister Mary only ever figured out ten of them.

SUPERHERO STAT

Frank Hawking's career meant that he was often away from home for months at a time as he took regular trips to Africa to carry out his research into tropical diseases. Stephen's sister Mary thought their father was like a bird that migrates in winter, returning home when the weather turned warmer! In 1950, Frank, after 11 years at the National Institute for Medical Research, became a department head when the important scientific research body moved to Mill Hill, on the northern edge of London. The family, in turn, made the move to St. Albans, a small city about 20 miles (30 km) north of Highgate.

LITTLE EINSTEIN

Hawking was eight when his family arrived in St. Albans. It is one of England's oldest cities, with a cathedral that dates back more than 1,700 years and even older foundations, built on the site of the Roman city of Verulamium.

The house the Hawkings moved into was big and rambling. For a family home, however, it had few luxuries and was always in need of repair. There was no proper heating—if people were cold, Frank Hawking simply insisted that they put on extra layers of clothes. One thing the Hawkings's home definitely had, however, was plenty of books. Visitors to the house reported that the family members usually had their head in a book, even when having their meals at the dining table.

Hawking attended St. Albans High School for Girls (which took boys up to the age of ten) and then

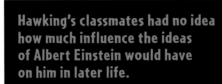

Hawking's classmates had no idea how much influence the ideas of Albert Einstein would have on him in later life.

Math Kit

When he was 16, Hawking and a group of his friends built themselves a computer out of parts of old clocks and a telephone switchboard. They named it LUCE—the Logical Uniselector Computing Engine—and it could carry out simple mathematical functions.

St. Albans, Hawking's childhood town, is famous for its grand cathedral as well as its Roman ruins.

Wow!

moved to St. Albans School. His untidy work and poor handwriting gave his teachers headaches, but, as if they knew what was to come, Hawking's classmates nicknamed him "Einstein."

When Hawking was 13, his father wanted him to try for a place at the prestigious Westminster School in London. As his parents were not wealthy, he needed to win a scholarship in order to attend. However, Hawking was sick at the time of the scholarship examination and did not take it. He later said that the education he got at St. Albans was just as good as he could have expected at Westminster.

When it came time to choose a university course, Hawking wanted to specialize in mathematics and physics. His father, however, was against this. The final decision to study physics and chemistry with just a little mathematics thrown in would eventually lead to Hawking having to develop the math skills he needed for his later research virtually on his own.

Chapter 2

FROM STUDENT TO DOCTOR

In March 1959, Hawking took the University of Oxford scholarship examinations, aiming to study natural sciences. As his parents well knew, an Oxford education would be expensive and the scholarship was vital.

To make things more difficult, Frank Hawking had been sent on a long-term assignment to India during his son's last year at high school. Hawking stayed behind with family friends while the rest of the Hawkings went abroad. The principal at St. Albans thought that Stephen should wait another year before taking the scholarship exams, but he decided to go ahead with them. A few days after completing the exams, Hawking received a telegram—he had the scholarship.

Hawking became an avid member of his college rowing team while at the University of Oxford.

In October 1959, at the age of 17, Hawking took up his place at University College, Oxford, where he specialized in physics in his natural sciences degree. He described the University of Oxford as being very "anti-work"—if you were naturally brilliant enough you would get a good degree, but actually working hard for one was frowned upon.

Easy Does It

Hawking calculated that over the three years he spent studying at Oxford he did about 1,000 hours of work—an average of an hour a day.

SUPERHERO STAT

The University of Oxford is recognized as being one of the top five universities in the world.

In his second year, Hawking took up rowing. He did not have the physical strength to row but he could be the cox, or leader, of the rowing team, steering and shouting out orders to the boat's eight rowers. Rowing gave Hawking a real sense of belonging and he became happier and more relaxed.

As the end of his time at Oxford approached, Hawking had been accepted for a place at Cambridge to study for his doctorate—but only if he secured a "first class" degree from Oxford. With the final exams looming, he started to study harder than ever before. When the results came in, Hawking was on the border between a first-class and a second-class degree. The examiners called him to an interview. Feeling confident, Hawking declared, "If I get a First, I shall go to Cambridge. If I receive a Second, I will remain at Oxford. So I expect that you will give me a First." He got his "First!"

DOCTOR HAWKING

Hawking moved to Cambridge to take up research in general relativity and cosmology—challenging subjects for someone with little mathematical background. He applied to work with the English astronomer Fred Hoyle, who was the greatest defender of what was known as the steady-state theory of cosmology.

The biggest question for cosmologists in the early 1960s was, did the universe have a beginning? Many scientists were opposed to the idea. They could not see how science could describe the event that created the universe. That was something that belonged to religion.

Zoom!

When Hawking graduated, scientists were wrestling with ideas about the origins of the universe.

It turned out that Hoyle could not take on any more students, so Hawking had to study under English physicist Dennis Sciama. Hawking had not heard of Sciama, but he would prove to be a strong supporter and Hawking came to enjoy the friendly and supportive environment Sciama created for his students.

Because Hawking had not done much math at school, and there had been little in his physics course at Oxford, Sciama suggested that he work on astrophysics. However, Hawking had come to Cambridge to study cosmology and that was what he was going to do. He read old textbooks on the

Blazing a Trail

When deciding between studying particle physics, which looks at the behavior of subatomic particles, or cosmology—not a popular subject at the time—Hawking chose cosmology because, he said, particle physics "seemed like botany. There were all these particles, but no theory."

In 1963, it seemed as if ALS might bring Hawking's career, and life, to an early end.

subject and traveled every week to lectures at King's College, London.

During his last year at Oxford, Hawking noticed that he was getting clumsy and sometimes had difficulty talking. When he went home for Christmas in 1962, his family saw something was wrong and persuaded him to see a doctor. Early in 1963, Hawking was diagnosed as having ALS, a condition that affects nerve cells in the brain and spinal cord, leading to gradual loss of all muscle control. The doctors predicted that Hawking would not live more than a few years.

LOVE AND AMBITION

During Hawking's first two years at Cambridge, his condition grew worse. He found it hard to get around and had to use a stick to help him walk. Dennis Sciama remembered how Hawking would often turn up to college with his head bandaged after a fall. His speech was affected, too, and even close friends struggled to understand what he was saying.

Around the same time he was diagnosed with ALS, Hawking met a woman named Jane Wilde at a New Year's Eve party in St. Albans. A few days later he invited her to his 21st birthday party. The two were soon seeing much more of each other and were engaged in October 1964. This was a turning point in Hawking's life. He realized that if he were going to get married, he would have to get a job, and that meant finishing his PhD, or doctorate. According to Hawking, "I started working for the first time in my life."

At one point, Hawking's father,

Pow!

In the mid 1960s, Hawking began to study the mysterious regions of space called black holes.

Frank, visited Dennis Sciama and asked if there was any way Stephen could complete his doctorate in less than three years. Sciama said this was impossible. However, he had seen what a big difference Jane Wilde had made to Hawking's outlook on life and Sciama really believed that he would find the determination to achieve his goal.

Another boost to Hawking's work was his meeting with English physicist Roger Penrose. Penrose had been applying his mathematical skills to studying what happened when a massive object, such as a star, collapses under its own gravity. Hawking was also working on some ideas about these mysterious objects. As it happened, Penrose's brother was a friend of Dennis Sciama, and Penrose and Hawking were introduced. They would form a partnership to study what became known as "black holes."

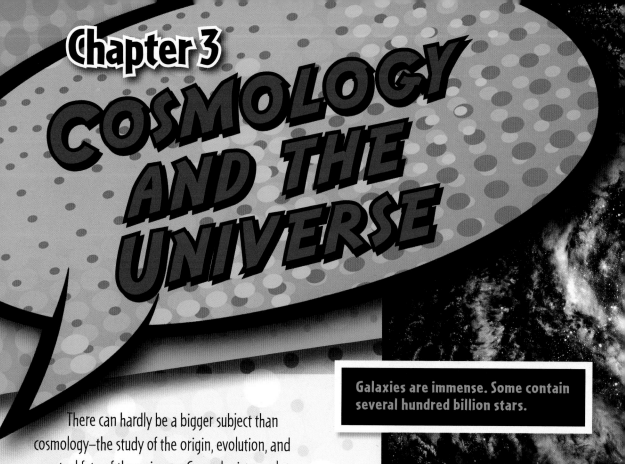

Chapter 3
COSMOLOGY AND THE UNIVERSE

Galaxies are immense. Some contain several hundred billion stars.

There can hardly be a bigger subject than cosmology–the study of the origin, evolution, and eventual fate of the universe. Cosmologists work to understand how the universe came into being, why it looks as it does now, and what will happen to it in the future. This is the subject to which Stephen Hawking would dedicate his life.

Cosmologists are not concerned with single stars and planets, or even galaxies. They want to know the answers to the big questions. How big is the universe? Where did it come from? Will it last forever? Is all we can see all that there is?

Our ideas about the structure of the universe changed in the 1920s, when astronomers such as the American Edwin Hubble began exploring space with powerful new telescopes. Hubble found that stars are not distributed evenly through space, but are gathered together in huge clusters called galaxies. By measuring the light from these galaxies, Hubble could figure out how fast they were moving. He expected that they would be moving randomly, with as many moving toward us as were moving away. To his surprise, Hubble found that not only were the galaxies moving away from us, but also the farther away they were the faster they were moving. The universe was expanding.

Big Bang Beginnings

Scientists have estimated that the big bang happened around 14 billion years ago. It took around another 400 million years for the first stars to form.

SUPERHERO STAT

EDWIN HUBBLE
ASTRONOMER

a 41

The astronomer Edwin Hubble was the first person to discover that the universe is expanding.

When Stephen Hawking went to Cambridge there were two conflicting ideas about the origins of the universe. One, called the steady-state theory, said that the universe expanded, but as it did so new matter was being created all the time, so the amount of matter in any particular region of space stayed more or less the same over time.

The other idea, called the big bang theory, said that the universe had begun as a tiny point of energy and had been expanding outward ever since. As no new matter was created, the galaxies were gradually moving apart from each other and space was becoming emptier. All the evidence we have today points toward the big bang theory being the right one.

BLACK HOLES REVEALED

In 1966, Hawking earned his PhD in physics. He did so by completing a piece of work called a dissertation, which was titled "Occurrence of Singularities in Cosmology." The dissertation built on Roger Penrose's work on black holes.

A black hole is a place in space where the force of gravity is so powerful that not even light can escape from it. The name "black hole" is usually credited to American physicist John Wheeler, who coined the term in a 1967 lecture.

Black holes form when a big star comes to the end of its life. The outer part of the star explodes out into space as a supernova, leaving the dense core, or center, of the star behind. When the star was active, the nuclear energy it produced was enough to keep the force of gravity from causing the star to collapse in on itself. Without that energy, the core of the star begins to collapse into a smaller and smaller space, becoming more and more dense until it forms a "singularity." This is a point in space that is infinitely small and infinitely dense. All of the matter that made up the core of the star is packed into a tiny point even smaller than an atom.

Whoosh!

Black holes are invisible—but we may be able to detect them from the matter that falls into them.

Big Bang Proof

Hawking and Penrose showed that if the description of the universe given by Albert Einstein's theory of general relativity was correct, then the universe must have begun with a singularity. The two physicists came up with mathematical proof that the universe had indeed begun with a "big bang" as the singularity exploded outward.

STAR CONTRIBUTION

The boundary marking the limits of a black hole is called the "event horizon." This is the distance from the singularity at which its gravitational pull is so strong that light itself is trapped by it. Since nothing can escape from within the event horizon, we cannot know what is happening inside it.

After completing his doctorate in 1966, Hawking was awarded a fellowship in theoretical physics at Gonville and Caius College, Cambridge. He and Penrose worked together on their joint ideas about singularities and the origins of the universe. Penrose had developed new mathematical techniques to explain how space and time are curved by a singularity. Hawking then took these ideas and applied them to the whole universe.

QUANTUM VERSUS RELATIVITY

For about a century, physics has been dominated by two great theories, or ideas, about how the universe works. The first of these, Einstein's theory of general relativity, looks at things on a grand scale, describing how gravity shapes the universe of space and time. The second, quantum mechanics, describes how the universe works on the very smallest scale, down to the size of atoms and even smaller.

Both theories work extremely well. They have been tested by observation and experiment to extraordinary levels of accuracy and each one of them seems to reflect the universe as it actually is. The problem facing physics is that the two theories just do not join up. The laws of relativity that govern the universe on the large scale do not apply on the small scale of quantum mechanics. The opposite is also true—quantum mechanics tells us nothing

All the matter and energy in the universe were created by the big bang, 14.6 billion years ago.

Super Small

When considering conditions in the early universe, Hawking was thinking on an incredibly small scale. At its very start, the universe was just a billion trillion trillionth of a centimeter across.

SUPERHERO STAT

Einstein's theories help us to understand how the universe works on a grand scale.

about the movements of galaxies. At the moment, there is no theory that successfully combines gravity with quantum mechanics.

It was Hawking's ambition to find a way to unite the two theories, especially through his studies of black holes and singularities. His and Penrose's results showed that Einstein's theory of general relativity predicted that the universe started as a singularity. However, they also showed that relativity does not apply in the immensely strong gravitational fields that were present in the early very small and dense universe. At this scale, quantum mechanics has to be taken into account.

Hawking developed the idea that the quantum creation of the universe could be imagined as being like bubbles of steam in boiling water, appearing and then disappearing. Some universes were like these bubbles, only expanding so far and then collapsing and vanishing again. These alternative universes would not last long enough for stars or galaxies to appear, and certainly not long enough for the development of intelligent life. Some bubbles, however, would grow big enough to avoid collapsing. They would go on expanding at an ever-increasing rate, with tiny irregularities in the bubble leading to the formation of planets, stars, galaxies, and life.

Chapter 4
DISCOVERIES AND PRIZES

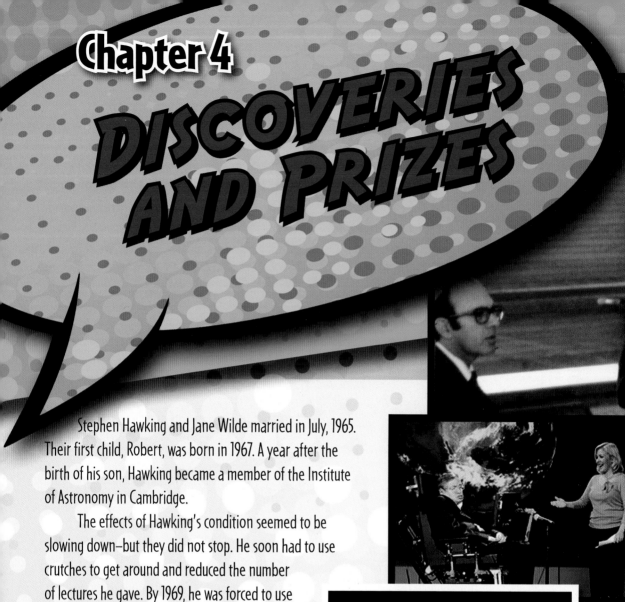

Stephen Hawking and Jane Wilde married in July, 1965. Their first child, Robert, was born in 1967. A year after the birth of his son, Hawking became a member of the Institute of Astronomy in Cambridge.

The effects of Hawking's condition seemed to be slowing down–but they did not stop. He soon had to use crutches to get around and reduced the number of lectures he gave. By 1969, he was forced to use a wheelchair. As he lost the ability to write things down, Hawking developed the remarkable talent of visualizing complex equations in his head.

In recent years, Hawking and his daughter, Lucy, have worked together to write a number of books for children.

Despite his physical setbacks, the next few years were exciting ones for Hawking. His daughter, Lucy, was born in 1970, and his research continued to bring attention. This was a hard time for Jane Hawking, though. She was struggling to complete her own PhD thesis at the same time as looking after a young son, an increasingly disabled

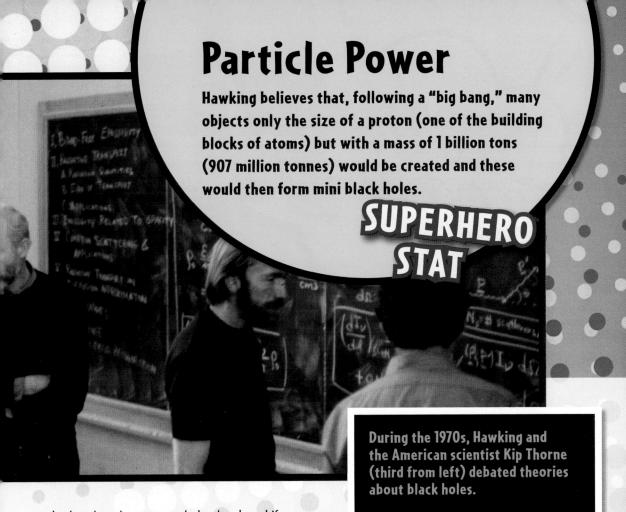

Particle Power

Hawking believes that, following a "big bang," many objects only the size of a proton (one of the building blocks of atoms) but with a mass of 1 billion tons (907 million tonnes) would be created and these would then form mini black holes.

SUPERHERO STAT

During the 1970s, Hawking and the American scientist Kip Thorne (third from left) debated theories about black holes.

husband, and now a new baby daughter. Life, however, was made much easier when, in 1971, Hawking won the annual international Gravity Research Foundation Award, with a piece on black holes.

Also in 1971, Hawking's investigations into the creation of the universe led him to predict that conditions at the beginning of a universe would be so extreme that matter would be forced into tiny superdense clumps, forming, in effect, "mini" black holes. The unique feature of mini black holes is that that while their immense mass and gravity mean that they are ruled by the laws of relativity, their minute size means that they are governed also by the laws of quantum mechanics.

Hawking then thought about how these mini black holes would interact with the space around them. In 1974, his calculations led him to a conclusion that at first he found so surprising he thought he must have made a mistake. Eventually, though, he came to believe he was right. A mini black hole would emit particles and eventually evaporate.

VANISHING BLACK HOLES

Hawking's findings about mini black holes were indeed surprising. Up until then it was thought that absolutely nothing got out of a black hole. Its powerfully concentrated gravity bent space and time to such a degree that nothing could escape from inside the event horizon. Hawking's calculations showed that a mini black hole would gradually lose mass and energy as particles escaped from it. How was this possible?

The answer is that the particles are not formed within the event horizon but just outside it. The laws of quantum mechanics allow the sharply curved space-time around the event horizon to cause tiny subatomic particles to form spontaneously. These particles form in pairs, one positive and one negative. Usually these particle pairs destroy each other in a fraction of a second. However, at the edge of a black hole event horizon it is possible for one of the pairs to escape while the other falls back into the black hole. The particle that enters

Wham!

Hawking believes that black holes emit radiation and gradually disappear altogether.

Radical Radiation

The idea of Hawking radiation and disappearing black holes was controversial at first. However, by the late 1970s, further research meant that Hawking's discovery came to be seen as a major breakthrough in physics.

STAR CONTRIBUTION

the black hole has negative energy. It is the flow of negative energy particles into the black hole that causes it to lose mass and eventually to disappear in a sudden burst of radiation. This has become known as "Hawking radiation."

In March 1974, a few weeks after publishing his findings about black holes, Hawking became a Fellow of the Royal Society in London. At the age of 32 he was one of the youngest scientists to have been given this honor.

Hawking's success in showing that evaporating black holes could exist spurred him on to try to find a way to combine the theory of general relativity with quantum theory. His first book, *The Large Scale Structure of Space-Time*, published in 1973, continued his work on Einstein's theory of general relativity and the existence of singularities.

AWARD WINNER

In 2009, President Barack Obama presented Hawking with the Presidential Medal of Freedom.

Recognition of Hawking's achievements followed quickly. Growing public interest in the mysterious black holes led to him making several appearances on television to talk about his ideas.

In 1975, the Royal Astronomical Society in London awarded Hawking the Eddington Medal, for outstanding work in astrophysics. That same year he went to Rome, where he received the Pius XI medal for exceptional scientific promise from Pope Paul VI. More prizes came Hawking's way in 1976, including the Maxwell medal, awarded by the Institute of Physics in London for his work in theoretical physics, and the Hughes medal, given by the Royal Society for "distinguished contributions to the application of general relativity to astrophysics."

In fall 1977, the University of Cambridge appointed Hawking to a professorship in gravitational physics. Rather than Doctor Hawking, he was now Professor Hawking. Then, two years later, came one of Hawking's greatest honors, when he was named Lucasian Professor of Mathematics at Cambridge, a distinguished position that had been

Math Master

Hawking became a professor of mathematics at Cambridge, one of the world's most prestigious universities, despite having received no formal math instruction since leaving school in St. Albans at the age of 17.

When Hawking became Lucasian Professor at Cambridge he was following in the footsteps of the great scientist Isaac Newton.

held by just 16 other people, including Isaac Newton. His first lecture as Lucasian Professor was called "Is the End in Sight for Theoretical Physics?"

Also in 1979, Hawking received the very first Albert Einstein medal, given by the Albert Einstein Society in Switzerland for scientific work related to Einstein's theories. Back in the United Kingdom, in 1982, Hawking became a Commander of the British Empire (CBE), a rank just below that of a knight. He was also made a Companion of Honor, which is given in recognition of exceptional national service. There can be no more than 65 living members of the order at one time.

In 2009, Hawking was presented with the Presidential Medal of Freedom, the highest honor that can be bestowed on a civilian in the United States. The one prize that continues to elude him, however, is the Nobel Prize for Physics.

Chapter 5

TRIALS AND TRIUMPHS

Zap!

Astronomers believe that an object in space called Cygnus X-1 is actually a star in orbit around a black hole.

At the same time as his research was taking him to the farthest reaches of the universe, Hawking's health was hampering him more and more, and putting increasing strain on his wife, Jane. When Hawking was appointed to a visiting professorship in 1975 at the California Institute of Technology (Caltech) in Pasadena, Jane suggested that one of Hawking's graduate students should come live with them and help care for him. Hawking agreed with this, and so student Bernard Carr traveled to California with the Hawkings. He was the first of many students who took on the role of Hawking's helper.

While at Caltech, Hawking made a bet with a fellow scientist, the American physicist Kip Thorne, that a mysterious object in space named Cygnus X-1 was not, as Thorne thought, a star orbiting around an unseen black hole. The prize was a magazine subscription. Hawking said that if black holes did not exist he would have wasted a lot of work, but at least he would enjoy his magazine! Eventually, in 1990, he conceded that Thorne was probably right and settled the bet.

STAR CONTRIBUTION

Endless Universe

In 1983, Hawking and American physicist Jim Hartle proposed the theory that the universe has no boundaries. They did this by combining ideas from quantum mechanics with general relativity. Hawking suggested comparing the universe to the surface of Earth. You can head off in any direction on Earth and never reach a point where it comes to an end. It is the same with the universe—except that Earth's surface is basically flat and two-dimensional, while the universe has four, or even more, dimensions.

By the late 1970s, Hawking could still feed himself and get out of bed but needed help with most other things. His speech had become slurred, and close family and friends would have to speak for him.

When they returned to Cambridge, Hawking and his wife argued with the university authorities about who should pay for the ramp he needed for his wheelchair. They also campaigned for better facilities and support at the university for students with disabilities.

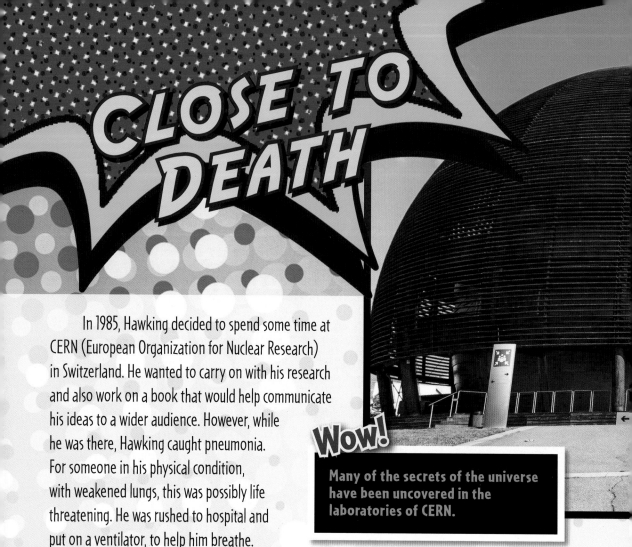

CLOSE TO DEATH

In 1985, Hawking decided to spend some time at CERN (European Organization for Nuclear Research) in Switzerland. He wanted to carry on with his research and also work on a book that would help communicate his ideas to a wider audience. However, while he was there, Hawking caught pneumonia. For someone in his physical condition, with weakened lungs, this was possibly life threatening. He was rushed to hospital and put on a ventilator, to help him breathe.

Wow!

Many of the secrets of the universe have been uncovered in the laboratories of CERN.

The doctors in the Swiss hospital thought Hawking was too far-gone to save and offered his wife, Jane, the option of turning off the ventilator machine to let him die. However, Jane refused and had him flown by air ambulance to Addenbrooke's Hospital, in Cambridge, where the doctors performed an emergency tracheostomy. This is a surgical procedure that involves cutting into the windpipe and inserting a tube that allows the person to breathe.

The operation was a success but it had meant cutting Hawking's vocal cords, making it impossible for him to speak. It also meant that he would now need round-the-clock care from a dedicated team of nurses for the rest of his life. Hawking has described the weeks

Beating the Odds

Doctors are actually at a loss to explain how Hawking has survived so long with ALS. Most people who contract the condition are diagnosed after the age of 50 and expected to die within 5 years. Hawking was diagnosed at the age of 21 and is still alive in his 70s.

SUPERHERO FACT

of intensive care that followed the operation as being the darkest days of his life.

In early November 1985, Hawking returned home from Addenbroke's Hospital. His poor health was making it difficult for him to work and now he could not speak at all. The only way he could communicate with other people was to spell out words by raising his eyebrows when somebody pointed to the correct letter on a spelling card.

Now in his 70s, Hawking still makes many public appearances.

FINDING A VOICE

A dedicated team work to ensure that Hawking's electronic equipment performs flawlessly.

Some hopeful news came from the United States. Walt Waltosz, a California computer programmer, had developed a program that allowed the user to select words on a screen and assemble them into sentences. An electronic voice synthesizer would then speak the words. Waltosz sent the program to Hawking.

The husband of one of Hawking's nurses was a computer engineer. He adapted a computer and synthesizer to Hawking's wheelchair so he could use the program. At first, Hawking selected his words with a handheld mouse. He now directs the program through a cheek muscle attached to a sensor. One small problem with the synthesizer was that it gave Hawking, who is English, an American accent, but he soon had fun opening his lectures with "Hello, please excuse my American accent."

If his computer were to stop working, Hawking would be cut off from the world. When he goes on a trip, there is far more to do than simply pack his passport and

Tools for Talking

The computer is just one piece of the total system Hawking depends on. This system includes not only the computer, but also the voice synthesizer, and a range of devices, including a USB hub, audio amplifier and voice interface, power modules, and the speaker through which his "voice" emerges.

Computer engineer Travis Bonifield holds a customized PC he designed specially for Hawking.

toothbrush. He travels with a large amount of backup hardware. Until recently, whenever Hawking went abroad, his assistants had to dismantle the communication system from his main wheelchair, which he uses only in the United Kingdom, and mount the equipment onto a folding travel wheelchair.

Today, Hawking has a fully equipped travel chair, as well as his regular wheelchair. This has great advantages. If he has a new system installed he can easily be moved from one chair to the other while engineers carry out the work, and also his assistants no longer need to dismantle and install the system on a different chair every time he travels. They can simply switch Hawking's laptop from chair to chair, while he can be moved by his experienced helpers in just a few moments, free to carry on with his research.

BOOK BREAKTHROUGH

In 1982, Hawking decided to write a book on cosmology that could be read by nonspecialists. He wanted to write something that people would buy at airports and take on vacation with them. By 1984, he had produced a first draft of *A Brief History of Time*.

This was the book Hawking had been working on during his visit to CERN in Switzerland, when his life-threatening pneumonia prevented him from carrying on.

Hawking feels strongly that as many people as possible should be able to read about his ideas.

When he was really sick, he despaired of ever finishing the book at all, but with the help of his new electronic voice he revized the work and it was published in spring 1988.

The launch party for the book's publication in the United States was held at the Rockefeller University in New York City. By all accounts, Hawking was full of energy and in a party mood, zipping around in his wheelchair from one guest to another. At one point, his wife, Jane, and his nurse were worried that he was getting so carried away he was going to wheel himself right into the East River!

Hawking the Recordbreaker

By May 1995, *A Brief History of Time* had been in *The Sunday Times* bestseller list in the United Kingdom for 237 weeks, breaking the previous record of 184 weeks and winning Hawking a place in the 1998 *Guinness Book of Records*. Since its publication, the book has sold more than 10 million copies worldwide and been translated into more than 40 languages.

The first print run of 40,000 copies sold out almost immediately and the book was reprinted and rushed into bookstores. This was well before the days when people could simply download a book onto their e-reader. By the summer of 1988, *A Brief History of Time* had sold half a million copies in the United States and been on the bestseller lists for four months.

In an interview, Hawking said that *A Brief History of Time* was the book he enjoyed writing most. A movie version of the book, directed by Errol Morris and produced by Steven Spielberg, premiered in 1992.

Action!

Movie director Steven Spielberg has been fascinated by space from an early age.

Chapter 6
A THEORY OF EVERYTHING

Many people were taken by surprise at how amazingly popular Hawking's books proved to be. In 2014, the film *The Theory of Everything* proved popular, too. It chronicled Hawking's relationship with his first wife, his diagnosis of ALS, and his success in science.

For a long time, Hawking has believed in the search for a "theory of everything," something that would unite quantum theory and relativity. *A Brief History of Time*, along with later books such as *The Universe in a Nutshell* and *The Grand Design*, illustrated Hawking's quest for science's Holy Grail: a single unifying theory that can combine general relativity (governing the universe on a large scale) with quantum mechanics (the instruction book for the infinitely small).

Everything we know about the universe is based around four fundamental properties–space, time, mass, and energy. Einstein's explanation for gravity is that it is a result of space-time being curved by the presence of mass and energy. In 1971, with his proposal for Hawking radiation, Hawking showed that sharply curved space-time could give rise to mass-energy (according to Einstein, mass and energy are just two different forms of the same thing).

Brain Stretchers!

Hawking thinks that one route toward a theory of everything might lie in something named "M-theory." This mystifying theory involves such mindbenders as 11 dimensions of space-time, multiple universes, superstrings, supergravity, and higher dimensional branes. Hawking explored these ideas in the book *The Grand Design*, written with American physicist Leonard Mlodinow in 2010.

SUPERHERO FACT

Zoom!

Some of the amazing ideas Hawking explores can often seem like pure science fiction.

So, if mass-energy curves space-time and curved space-time causes mass-energy to appear, which came first? If they both appeared together simultaneously in the big bang, then what did they arise from? What in the universe could be more basic than space, time, mass, and energy? No one knows the answer to the "which came first?" question, or even if the question itself is meaningful in any way that we could understand. "To understand the universe at the deepest level," Hawking says, "we have to understand why is there something rather than nothing. 'Why do we exist?'"

In the 1980s, Hawking declared that there was a 50 percent chance that a theory unifying relativity and quantum mechanics would be found by 2000. Unfortunately, that has not happened.

BLACK HOLE BETS

Professor Roger Penrose has worked with Hawking for more than 40 years.

The strain of dealing with her husband's increasing needs eventually became too much for Jane Hawking. In 1995, the couple divorced and Hawking remarried, this time to Elaine Mason, who was one of his nurses.

Through all of this, Hawking continued his researches and efforts to reach a wider audience for his ideas. He was still working with Roger Penrose, and in 1993 the two gave a series of lectures on "The Nature of Space and Time." Also in 1993, Hawking published a popular collection of essays and interviews called *Black Holes and Baby Universes and Other Essays.* This was followed by a six-part television series, *Stephen Hawking's Universe*, which appeared in 1997.

STAR CONTRIBUTION

Idea Challenger

Hawking and other talented physicists may have plenty of fun making bets on these big questions, but it does not make them any less important. Hawking's idea that black holes could destroy information challenged some of the most important ideas of quantum physics.

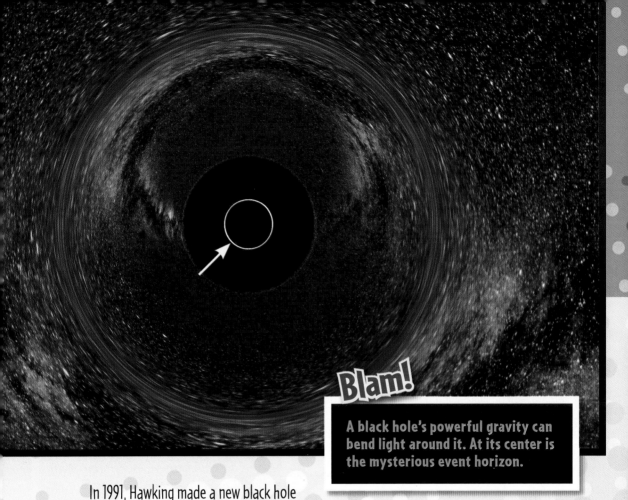

A black hole's powerful gravity can bend light around it. At its center is the mysterious event horizon.

In 1991, Hawking made a new black hole bet with Kip Thorne—and another Caltech physicist, John Preskill. Thorne and Preskill thought it was possible for a singularity to occur outside a black hole—a so-called "naked singularity." Hawking, backed up by Roger Penrose, said that this could not happen. In 1997, Hawking conceded the bet on what he named a "technicality," saying that naked singularities could form—but only under very special conditions.

Almost immediately afterward, Preskilll made another bet with Hawking, this time concerning what happens to the information that is hidden behind a black hole's event horizon. Preskill bet that with the right kind of technology the information could be recovered from the radiation emitted as the black hole evaporated, while Hawking said the information would be destroyed. This time Thorne sided with Hawking. In 2004, Hawking outlined some new ideas he had about black holes that supported the conclusion that information loss does not occur after all. Again, he had to concede that Preskill might be right.

SPACE MAN

In 2007, at the age of 65, Hawking visited the Kennedy Space Center in Florida. There, he was given the chance to fly on a Boeing 727, which had been modified to give people, such as astronauts, training in weightlessness. During a two-hour flight over the Atlantic, the airplane made a series of rapid climbs and dives that allowed Hawking and the others onboard to experience 25-second bursts of weightlessness. Fortunately, the interior of the airplane was padded to avoid any injuries!

After the flight Hawking was thrilled by the adventure, saying, "The zero-G [gravity] part was wonderful and the higher-G part was no problem. I could have gone on and on. Space, here I come!"

Hawking believes that private space vehicles will make space accessible

Hawking was absolutely thrilled by his experience of zero gravity aboard a modified airplane.

SUPERHERO FACT

Funny Physicist

An appearance on *The Simpsons* gave Hawking the chance to demonstrate his great sense of humor. When Principal Skinner tries to interpret for him, Hawking stops him with a sharp "Silence! I don't need anyone to talk for me—except this voicebox ... ."

www.goZeroG.com

Hawking gave a series of lectures in praise of space travel to mark NASA's 50th anniversary in 2008.

to a greater number of people and he firmly intends to take his place on one of the first commercial flights into space. He has said that he does not believe the human race has a future unless it goes into space–in fact, he thinks the human race cannot survive another 1,000 years if it fails to make the leap into space. "Not to leave planet Earth would be like castaways on a desert island not trying to escape," he said. "Sending humans to other planets ... will shape the future of the human race in ways we don't yet understand."

In the fictional world, Hawking has already been into space. In 1993, he made a famous guest appearance on the television series *Star Trek: The Next Generation* as a hologram of himself playing poker with the android Commander Data, Albert Einstein, and Isaac Newton. He has also appeared as himself on the sitcoms *The Simpsons* and *The Big Bang Theory*.

LOOK TO THE FUTURE

Hawking's health is a constant concern. In April 2009, a gravely sick Hawking, who had retired after 30 years as Lucasian Professor of Mathematics, was rushed to the hospital but made a full recovery. He has reached his 70s with a disease that should have killed him by the age of 25. He says, "The doctor who diagnosed me with ALS told me it would kill me in two or three years. All my life, I have lived with the threat of an early death. So I hate wasting time."

In 2012, it was revealed that Hawking had taken part in trials for a new headband-style device named the iBrain, designed to pick up waves of electrical brain signals. He still works hard as a scientist, founding the Center for Theoretical Cosmology (CTC) and acting as Director of Research at the Department of Applied Mathematics and Theoretical Physics (DAMTP), both at the University of Cambridge.

Science Superstar!

Hawking's contributions to science have been immense. He has used Einstein's theory of general relativity to show how the universe began as a single point. He has investigated the properties of superdense black holes, even showing how they might evaporate and vanish in a burst of radiation. And he has shown how tiny variations in the conditions at the beginning of the universe have given rise to the stars and galaxies and made it possible for life, including us, to appear.

STAR CONTRIBUTION

Bang!

Hawking has fired the imaginations of many with his ideas about the workings of the universe.

Hawking continues to develop his theories about black holes and his hopes of being able to unite gravity with the forces at work in quantum mechanics. He even wonders if there really are such things as black holes. Instead of an event horizon, Hawking proposes an "apparent horizon," which instead of trapping matter and energy forever only imprisons them for a while, before eventually releasing them in a changed form. These are ideas that have developed over the 40 years since his first proposal of Hawking radiation.

Quantum theory, Hawking believes, "enables energy and information to escape from a black hole." Just how this process works will require a theory that successfully merges gravity with the other fundamental forces of nature that work on an atomic level—a goal that physicists, including Hawking, have struggled to achieve for nearly a century. As Hawking says, it "remains a mystery."

Glossary

astrophysics the study of the physical makeup of planets, stars, galaxies, and other objects in space

big bang the rapid expansion of the universe from an infinitely small, infinitely dense point at the beginning of time

black hole a region in space where matter has become so concentrated and the force of gravity so intense that nothing can escape from it, not even light

cosmology the branch of science that studies the origin of the universe, how it has developed, and what might happen to it in the future

event horizon the boundary line around a black hole that marks where the gravitational pull becomes strong enough to trap light. Nothing can be detected inside the event horizon.

galaxies systems of billions of stars. The galaxy our sun belongs to is called the Milky Way.

general relativity a theory put forward by the scientist Albert Einstein that explains that gravity is caused by the bending of space by the matter within it

gravitational fields the space around an object where the effects of its gravity can be felt

gravity the force of attraction that exists between objects—the more matter an object contains, the greater the pull of gravity it exerts

Hawking radiation radiation produced by a black hole due to particles being created just outside the event horizon

mass-energy mass (the amount of matter in something) representing a definite amount of energy

mini black holes black holes smaller than an atom, which would have to obey the laws of quantum mechanics. None have yet been proven to exist.

naked singularity a singularity that is thought to exist outside a black hole event horizon

quantum mechanics the branch of physics that deals with the behavior of particles on the scale of atoms and even smaller

singularity a point in which space is infinitely curved and matter infinitely dense

space-time the idea, put forward by Albert Einstein, that space and time should be considered as a single four-dimensional property that is affected by mass and energy

steady-state theory a theory (now abandoned) that proposed that new matter was constantly being created as the universe expanded

subatomic smaller than an atom

supernova a star that suddenly increases greatly in brightness as a massive explosion throws most of its mass out into space

theoretical physics the branch of physics that uses mathematics to explain how the universe works rather than carrying out experiments

universe all the matter and energy that exists and the space in which it exists

For More Information

Books

Fleisher, Paul. *Relativity and Quantum Mechanics: Principles of Modern Physics* (Secrets of the Universe). Minneapolis, MN: Lerner Publications, 2002.

Hawking, Lucy, and Stephen Hawking. *George's Secret Key to the Universe.* New York, NY: Simon & Schuster, 2007.

Jackson, Ellen. *The Mysterious Universe: Supernovae, Dark Energy, and Black Holes.* Boston, MA: Houghton Mifflin Harcourt, 2008.

Pohlen, Jerome. *Albert Einstein and Relativity for Kids.* Chicago, IL: Chicago Review Press, 2012.

Websites

See a timeline for the big bang at:
www.esa.int/Our_Activities/Space_Science/So_how_did_everything_start

For everything a young astronomer needs to know, go to:
http://starchild.gsfc.nasa.gov/docs/StarChild/StarChild.html

Discover a galaxy of information about black holes at:
http://curious.astro.cornell.edu/blackholes.php

Index